THE WORLD HERITAGE

PREHISTORIC ROCK ART

UNESCO

CHILDRENS PRESS®

CHICAGO

Table of Contents

Library of Congress Cataloging-in-Publication Data

Terzi, Marinella.
  [Arte rupestre prehistorico. English]
  Prehistoric rock art / by Marinella Terzi.
    p. cm. — (The World heritage)
  Translation of: El arte rupestre prehistorico.
  Includes index.
  Summary: Discusses the subject matter, techniques, and cultural significance of the paintings and engravings made on rocks, both inside caves and in the open air, by primitive people around the world.
  ISBN 0-516-08379-1
  1. Rock paintings—Juvenile literature. 2. Art, Prehistoric—Juvenile literature. [1. Cave paintings. 2. Rock paintings. 3. Art, Prehistoric. 4. Art appreciation.]
I. Title. II. Series.
GN799.P4T4713 1992
709'.01'1—dc20
                                             92-7504
                                                CIP
                                                      AC

El Arte Rupestre Prehistorico: © INCAFO S.A./Ediciones S.M./UNESCO 1990
Prehistoric Rock Art: © Childrens Press,® Inc./UNESCO 1992

ISBN (UNESCO) 92-3-102599-6
ISBN (Childrens Press) 0-516-08379-1

Prehistoric Rock Art

How did the human race begin? This question has puzzled us for ages. We know that there was a hominid—or human-like—species living in Africa nearly four million years ago. Scientists have named it Australopithecus. Much later, around 1,600,000 B.C., a hominid called Homo erectus *appeared in Asia and Africa. This species is also known as Pithecanthropus.* Homo erectus *was a meat eater and so needed cutting tools to butcher animals. The first tools made of flint are from that time.*

From about 100,000 B.C., remnants of a more advanced human, Neanderthal, have been found in Asia, Africa, and Europe. Around the same time, our direct ancestors, Homo sapiens sapiens, *appeared in Africa. The structure of their bodies is much like that of modern humans.* Homo sapiens sapiens *had spread into Europe and Asia by 40,000 years ago. In Europe, they have been called Cro-Magnon. These are the people who created the first works of art—little figurines and drawings at first, and later, paintings on stone.*

The Magic of the Hunt
Scenes of animals and hunting are the major subjects in prehistoric rock art. Early peoples may have had a magical belief that prey could be captured more easily if its image were "captured" first. As these photos show, the styles vary considerably, depending on where the paintings are found. Painting methods were probably passed on from masters to apprentices. The top photo shows a detail of a painting on stone in Alta, Norway, from the later Neolithic period. Below is a deer's head from Altamira, Spain, painted in the Paleolithic era.

Daily Life in Prehistoric Times

Hominids needed to develop new abilities to cope with the hardships of their environment. They began to use their sense of sight more and more, and their sense of smell less and less. They had to be alert at all times, always ready to catch or gather food. When they stood on their hind legs, their front limbs were free to make and handle whatever tools they needed, especially those used for hunting. And so, after long ages of development, our own type of humans, *Homo sapiens sapiens*, spread throughout the world.

These first human beings appeared during the Paleolithic Era, or Old Stone Age. This was a period that lasted some two million years, until about 10,000 B.C.

The climate during the Paleolithic Era was much different than today's climate. A series of Ice Ages, or glaciations, occurred throughout Paleolithic times. Glaciers—huge masses of ice—covered much of the earth.

In between glaciations were periods of warmer weather, called interglacials. In Africa the Ice Ages were much milder, but they produced heavy rainfall.

People in the Paleolithic Era would take shelter at the entrances of caves. To get the food they needed, they hunted, fished, and gathered plants. They protected their bodies with the skins of the animals they hunted.

It was often hard simply to survive. People had to deal with difficult childbirths and with illnesses they barely understood. They had to protect themselves against wild beasts. The population was therefore sparse.

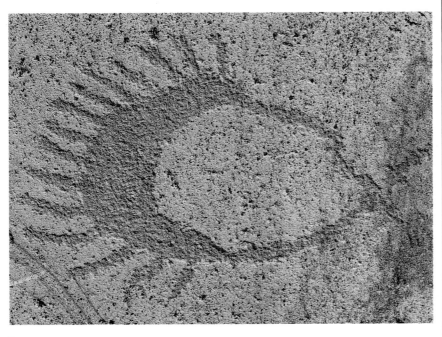

Descendants of the First Australians

Many settlements that date as far back as 25,000 years have been found in Kakadu National Park, Australia (*opposite page, top*). The present inhabitants still practice many traditional arts. In the photo at the left is a rock painting at Alta, Norway. The map (*right*) shows the locations of the places mentioned in this book. They are World Heritage sites, chosen by UNESCO for preservation.

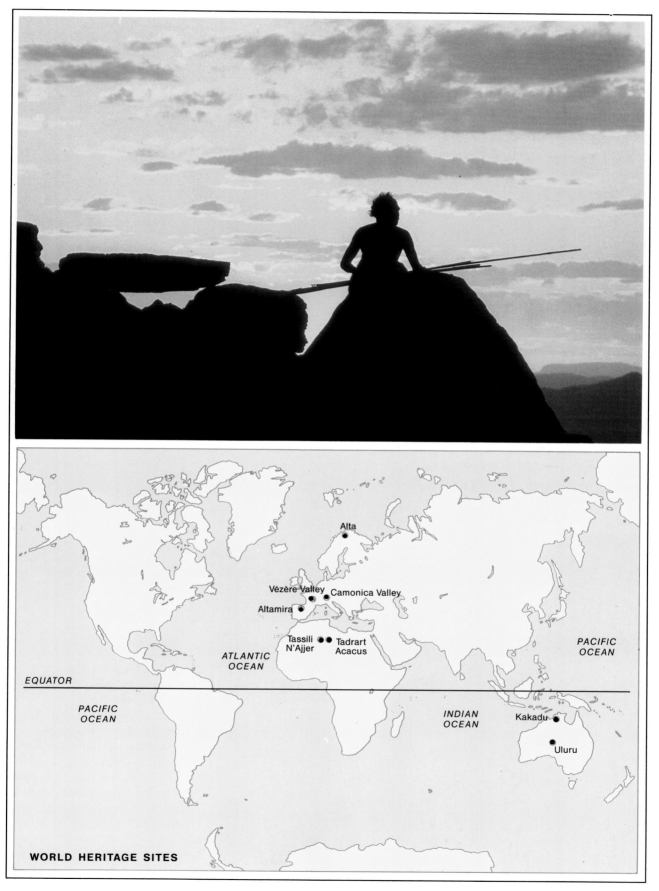

WORLD HERITAGE SITES

Alta

Vézère Valley   Camonica Valley
Altamira

Tassili   Tadrart
N'Ajjer   Acacus

PACIFIC
OCEAN

ATLANTIC
OCEAN

EQUATOR

PACIFIC
OCEAN

INDIAN
OCEAN

Kakadu

Uluru

The first tools were made of stone, wood, bone, and shells. During Paleolithic times, people made tools out of chipped stone. They used rocks broken from cliffs or pebbles gathered from streams. Stone was easy to shape by chipping, and it resisted scratches.

After the last Ice Age, the climate changed. Now a much gentler climate prevailed. But rainfall also decreased, causing severe dryness in many places. With the change in climate came the birth of agriculture. Instead of a nomadic life of hunting, people settled down to tend crops and built more solid houses. Usually, people settled next to rivers.

This change—from a wandering life to a settled life—marked the beginning of the Mesolithic Era. This period lasted from about 10,000 to 9000 B.C. in the Near East, and to about 4000 B.C. in Europe. Next came the Neolithic Era, lasting until around 3000 B.C.

Religious Motivation in Art

Once our early ancestors developed to a certain point, they began to create works of art. The earliest art objects may have been made for religious purposes. In many cases, the art may have been related to magic.

In today's way of thinking, an artist produces art to express personal ideas, thoughts, or feelings. But Paleolithic art objects were part of rituals and ceremonies related to birth, death, and fertility. The artists faced the same problems and hardships as the other people in their group. In such small societies, it was not likely that there were people dedicated only to art.

Between 30,000 and 20,000 B.C., the first figurines of humans were made out of stone, bone, and ivory. Some of them clearly represent women. Others appear to be youths or stylized forms.

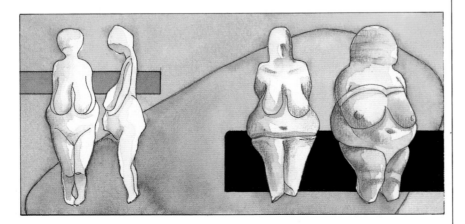

Art for Worship
The first works of art may have had a religious purpose. They were not made simply for personal expression, but as a part of rituals associated with birth, death, and fertility. The female figurines represented in the drawing (*left*) were created about 20,000 B.C. The photo at the right shows an image on rock from the Neolithic period found in the Tassili N'Ajjer, Algeria.

Rock Art

Glaciers still covered great parts of northern Europe when humans made the first paintings, engravings, and reliefs on rock walls. Using the carbon-14 method, these works can be dated between 25,000 and 10,000 B.C. (See explanation of carbon-14 dating on page 24.) This type of art reached its peak beginning about 15,000 B.C.

Most of these works were created by people who were talented artists. They used rapid strokes and various techniques of coloring and shading. By studying the many styles in rock art, we can tell that skills were passed on from masters to apprentices.

There are some paintings of people, as well as some symbols that we don't understand. But most of the paintings show figures of animals. It could be that the people believed their hunting would be more successful if the prey's image were captured in a painting.

The paintings are generally multi-colored. Most were painted in various shades of red, black, and yellow. The artists made the colors by mixing such substances as manganese, ocher, and charcoal with animal fat. They applied the colors to the walls with sticks or reeds, with their hands, or by blowing the ground-up pigment onto the rock wall. Sometimes they used brushes.

Engravings were carved with flint or other stone tools. Flint tools were also used to carve sculptures. One reason the paintings have lasted so long is because of the water in the caves. It contains lime (calcium oxide), and the lime has fossilized the paintings over the years. In other words, the paintings have gradually turned to stone.

Timeline of Prehistory

4 million years ago: Australopithecus appears

From 2 million years ago until 10,000 B.C.: Paleolithic Age

1,600,000 years ago: Homo erectus appears

100,000 years ago: Neanderthal and Homo sapiens sapiens appear

32,000 years ago: Homo sapiens sapiens (modern humans) are the only type of humans

From 10,000 to 9000 B.C. (to 4000 B.C. in Europe): Mesolithic Age

From the Mesolithic to around 3000 B.C.: Neolithic Age

From 3000 to 1100 B.C.: Bronze Age

From 1100 B.C. to the present: Iron Age

Rites of Yesterday and Today
At Kakadu National Park, more than one thousand sites with prehistoric art have been counted. One of them, Nourlangie Rock, is shown in the top photo. Australians say it represents Barginj, wife of the Lightning Spirit. Below it is an everyday scene among the people of Kakadu: a mother and her two children collect mollusks in the brackish waters that result when sea water and fresh water mix during the flood season.

The Rock that Hides a Secret

Uluru National Park in Australia's central desert covers about 512 square miles (132,500 hectares). The park is made up of wide expanses of sand, dunes, and desert formed by deposits from streams. Rising from this desert is the famous monolith of Ayers Rock, shown in the photo, which reaches a height of 2,845 feet (867 meters). Its top is almost flat. There are valuable and unique stone paintings on Ayers Rock, some of them around 10,000 years old. However, they are located in one of the three zones reserved exclusively for the native people. Tourists and photographers are not allowed to enter. The natural features of Uluru are just as important as the cultural. Its spectacular formations are of great interest to geologists who study the structure and chemistry of the earth. Biologists are just as interested in the national park as an ecosystem. It is home to many fascinating animal and plant species. At the same time, the native communities contribute their great cultural and religious heritage. "This is one land, one law, one people." That Anangu phrase sums up the sense of life in the heart of Australia.

The hunting of animals is one of the most common themes in the paintings and engravings. Sometimes there are figures of animals that barely existed in the artist's area. This may mean that the hunters were trying for rarer forms of prey.

In many cases, the painters took advantage of parts of the rock that jutted out. An animal painted on such a spot seemed to jut out, too. They even used natural features of the rocks, such as water trickles, to show wounds in the animals. Such techniques can be seen in Altamira and other Paleolithic caves.

In some caves, there are paintings painted on top of other paintings. Either they were created at different times or were deliberately made that way to to give an impression of depth.

Many cave paintings were done far from the entrance to a cave. This tells us that the people of that time used fire and knew how to control it. They used torches to light their way along the lengthy underground corridors. Remains of torches have been found in various Paleolithic sites. There were also stone lamps that were probably set at intersections or in front of decorated areas. These lamps did not give off much light, but they could last a long time. It has been determined that 10.5 ounces (300 grams) of animal fat could produce twenty-four hours of light.

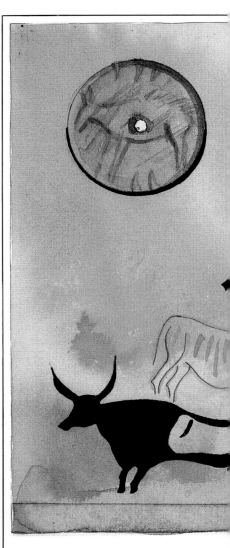

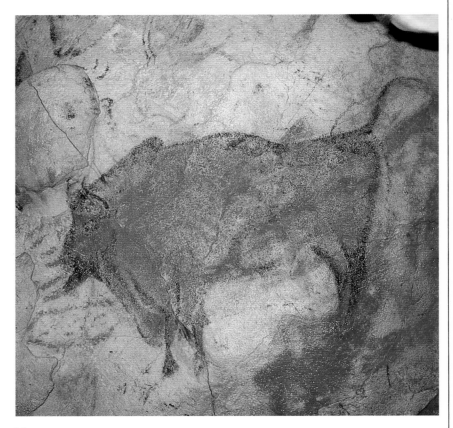

Fine Artistic Techniques

Prehistoric artists used excellent techniques. They often took advantage of raised areas on rocky walls to make their figures seem more real. Sometimes they accented the outlines of drawings by engraving them with a burin (a pointed flint tool) and filling in with black. These two techniques can be seen in the photos at the left and right. The painting on the left is from Altamira, Spain. The one on the right is from Lascaux Cave, in the Vézère Valley, France.

Caves in the Vézère Valley

Scattered throughout the Vézère Valley, in the French region of Aquitaine, are traces of the humans who lived there thousands of years ago. In the valley are 147 prehistoric sites and 25 decorated caves. The most famous is Lascaux Cave. It contains hundreds of paintings, some outlined with strokes made by a pointed flint tool called a burin. Some drawings are made on top of others, indicating that they were made at more than one time.

Animals of the time are the main subjects in the pictures. The artists took advantage of irregularities in the rocks to add some depth or relief. Their colors were yellow, different shades of ocher, and black.

One of the most interesting chambers in Lascaux Cave is the Room of the Bulls. One of the bulls painted there is 18 feet (5.5 meters) long.

Kakadu National Park

This Australian park is in the region of Arnhem Land, 185 miles (300 kilometers) east of the city of Darwin. More than 2,300 square miles (6,000 square kilometers) in area, the park is comprised of many different types of land. There are mangrove swamps and flooded plains, inhabited by a great population of aquatic birds. There is also a rocky plateau, with mountain masses as high as 1,640 feet (500 meters). Several human settlements up to 25,000 years old have been discovered on this plateau. There is evidence that the first inhabitants of Australia came from Asia at least 40,000 years ago.

Stone axes with ground cutting edges, about 20,000 years old, have been found in excavations in this region. They are the most ancient relics unearthed so far.

Prehistoric art appears in more than a thousand sites in Kakadu National Park. Some of the paintings show events or activities common in the community. Other pictures were painted for religious purposes, to obtain blessings for the group. Most of them are in shades of ocher and are quite well preserved, since the native people themselves have been in charge of taking care of them.

The present inhabitants, the Lardil, are direct descendants of the area's prehistoric residents. They are very interested in preserving their heritage. However, the paintings are now in danger of deteriorating, due mainly to the dust produced by traffic to the sites.

An Assortment of Animals
The Room of the Bulls is one of the most fascinating parts of Lascaux Cave in the Vézère Valley. This valley in the French region of Aquitaine, already inhabited 100,000 years ago, has 147 sites and 25 decorated caves. The best known is Lascaux Cave. (*Top*) A bull and a horse in Lascaux Cave. (*Bottom*) A rock painting of a turtle in Kakadu, Australia. Turtles were eaten by the inhabitants of the area.

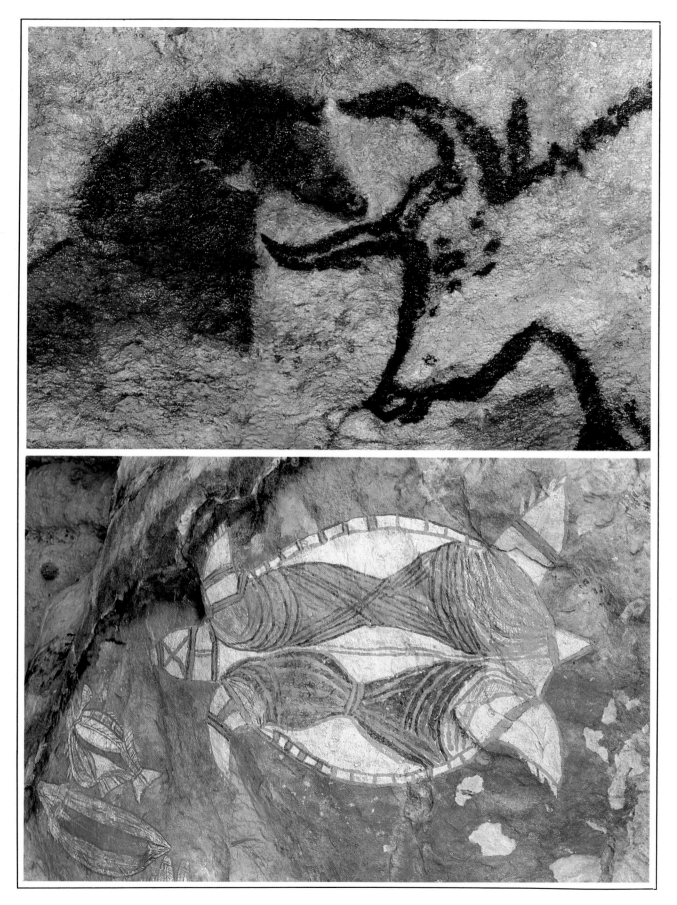

The Caves of Altamira

The caves of Altamira are in northern Spain, near Santillana del Mar in the Cantabrian Mountains. A hunter from the region discovered the caves in the middle of the nineteenth century. When the Marquis of Sautuola heard about them, he guessed that there might be something interesting inside. He visited the caves several times, but it was his daughter Maria who first discovered the famous bison on the ceiling in 1879.

The caves, located in a limestone plateau, are made up of a number of passageways and rooms, with a total length of 885 feet (270 meters). People probably lived in them as early as 30,000 B.C. But the many stone tools around the entrance indicate that the heaviest period of settlement was around 13,500 B.C. The twenty impressive multi-colored figures on the ceiling of the main room date from that time.

Bison, horses, deer, and wild boar are the subjects of the paintings. The artists used raised parts of the rock to make the animals look even more realistic. Some of the animals' bodies stand out like relief sculptures. They are painted in various shades of ocher, red, and black.

Three types of pictures appear in the caves: animals, human beings, and unknown symbols or designs. The animal figures may represent dead animals lying in a corral after being driven into a slaughter area. The caves of Altamira are now closed to the public to preserve the paintings.

A Ceiling Full of Bisons

The caves of Altamira, near Santillana del Mar, Spain, are closed to the public now to assure their preservation. The caves were inhabited most heavily around 13,500 B.C. With all their rooms and winding corridors, the caves' total length is 885 feet (270 meters). The most outstanding features are the twenty figures on the ceiling of the main room, painted in ocher, red, and black tones. It must have taken quite a bit of effort for the artists to have painted them, since they would have had to work in a very uncomfortable position.

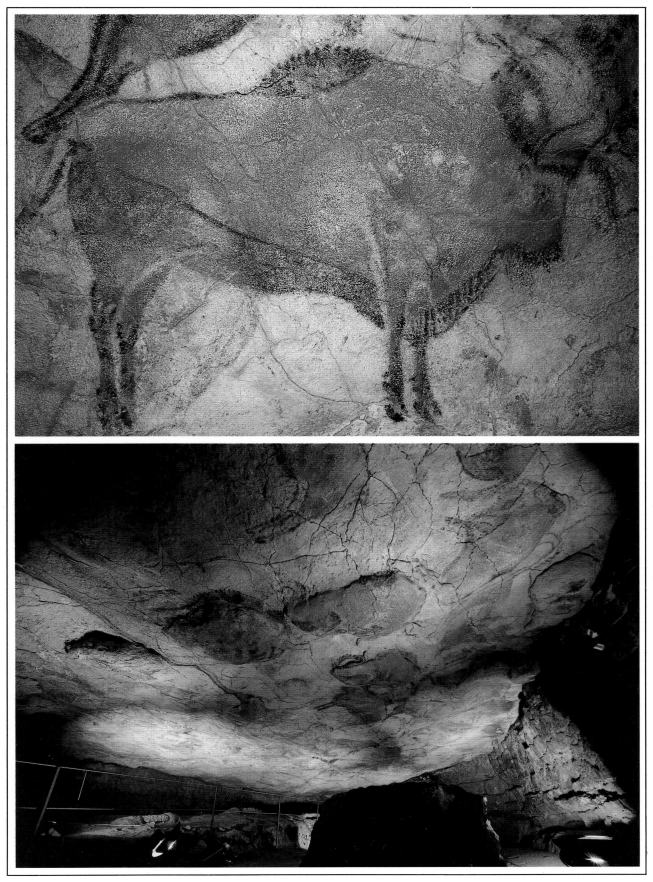

Struggle Against the Desert

The Tassili N'Ajjer is a long, flat rock, about 430 miles long and 62 miles wide (700 by 100 kilometers), in the southeast corner of Algeria. On it are more than 15,000 paintings, engravings, and other archaeological remains. They are vivid evidence of the diverse civilizations that have lived in the area, from the Saharan Neolithic era until quite recent times. The Tassili N'Ajjer is valuable to geologists and archaeologists. But it is also of great interest to biologists. It contains Mediterranean plants and animals that defy the area's tendency to turn into a desert.

Tassili N'Ajjer

Imagine a single, flat rock about 435 miles (700 kilometers) long and 62 miles (100 kilometers) wide, and almost 1.25 miles (2,000 meters) high. That is the Tassili N'Ajjer. It rises in the southeastern corner of Algeria, in the heart of the Sahara Desert of North Africa.

Wind and storms have worn away its clayey material, leaving unusual formations. This peculiar terrain is remarkable for its biology as well as its geology. Its plants and animals are similar to those in lands close to the Mediterranean Sea. They serve as a reminder of the past, of a time when the arid Sahara was lush and green.

Besides all this, the Tassili N'Ajjer is an archaeological site rich with prehistoric art. On its rock faces, there are more than 15,000 paintings, engravings, and other archaeological remnants. Together, they are a priceless testimony to the many civilizations that have lived in the area. There are paintings from the Saharan Neolithic period all the way up to recent times.

Archaeologists—scientists who study remains from past civilizations—have found that people have lived in this part of the Sahara region for over 7,000 years. Through the centuries, the dwellers have had to adjust to an ever more arid climate. As conditions changed, so did the people's way of life.

Several different styles of paintings are found in the Tassili N'Ajjer, each made in a different time period:

The Might of the Wind
The clayey material of the Tassili N'Ajjer has been worn away by winds and storms. This erosion has left some unusual formations, such as those in the photo at the right. At the left is one of the engravings at the Tassili N'Ajjer. It depicts a goat, an animal very abundant in the region.

Realistic period. These are the oldest paintings, created about 6000 B.C. They are pictures of wild animals of the savanna.

Period of round-headed beings. These paintings, often very small or very large, show beings with round and exaggerated heads. Whether they represent people or spirits or both is not known. They date from about 6000 to 4000 B.C.

Cattle herdsmen period. Most of the paintings at the Tassili N'Ajjer are in this style, used between about 4000 and 1200 B.C. There are many pictures of cattle and sheep and of people doing everyday chores.

Horse period. This period lasted from about 1200 B.C. to the end of the B.C. era. It is marked by scenes of horse-drawn chariots and of people riding on horseback. This might be explained by the inhabitants' contacts with Egypt and other North African cultures bordering the Mediterranean.

Camel period. From A.D. 300 to the present. Artists started making this kind of painting at a time when camels began to be used instead of horses. Along with the paintings are words written in Tifinagh, a form of writing still used by the present-day Tuareg people of the area.

Camels on the Rocks
The paintings at the Tassili N'Ajjer are divided into five styles, depending on the dates when they were created. The art in the bottom photo belongs to the camel period, from A.D. 300 to the present time. It was in this era that the camel replaced the horse. Paintings from the camel period usually have inscriptions in Tifinagh characters, a form of writing still used today by the Tuaregs. The photo above shows some of the clayey mountain masses in the area.

How Does Carbon-14 Dating Work?

The carbon-14 method was discovered in 1949 by the American physicist Willard Frank Libby. Using this method, scientists can discover the age of objects that are many thousands of years old. The test can be done on any organic material—that is, anything that was once alive.

All living things—animals and plants—contain the element carbon. Plants take in carbon dioxide and also a form of carbon called carbon-14. When animals eat plants, they take in the plant's carbon, too. While animals and plants are alive, the carbon-14 inside them is constantly breaking down. But they are constantly taking in more carbon-14 at the same time. Thus, the amount of carbon-14 inside an animal or plant stays the same as long as it's alive.

When something dies, it stops taking in carbon-14. But the carbon-14 inside it keeps breaking down just as it always did. As each atom of carbon-14 breaks down, a tiny "radioactive" particle shoots out.

We know that carbon-14 has a "half-life" of about 5,700 years. That's how long it takes for one-half the original amount of carbon-14 to break down. After another 5,700 years, one-quarter of it is left; in 5,700 more years, one-eighth is left, and so on. The number of radioactive particles shooting out of an object tells how much carbon-14 is still left in it.

With an instrument called a Geiger counter, scientists can count these particles. Once they know how much carbon-14 remains in the object, they can determine its age. After about 50,000 years, almost all the carbon-14 is gone. Thus, carbon-14 dating can be used to find the age of organic material that is up to 50,000 years old.

Fur, antlers, clothing, and wood are all objects whose age can be discovered using carbon-14 dating.

The artists' descendants — the Ajjer Tuaregs — are more bound to their ancient traditions than other Tuaregs are. They are also more independent. They lead a nomadic life, raising camels, goats, and sheep.

Rock Art Sites at Tadrart Acacus

The Tassili N'Ajjer region extends naturally across the Algerian border into southwestern Libya. There, at Tadrart Acacus, is a rocky mountain mass measuring almost 100 square miles (more than 250 square kilometers).

There, too, are found thousands of engravings and rock paintings. Some of them are older than the ones at the Tassili N'Ajjer, dating as far back as 12,000 B.C. Their styles are very different, depending on when they were made.

Experts have divided the art at Tadrart Acacus into the same periods as the paintings at the Tassili N'Ajjer:

> Realistic (possibly 12,000 to 7000 B.C.)
> Round-headed beings (7000 to 4000 B.C.)
> Cattle (4000 to 1200 B.C.)
> Horse (1200 B.C. to first century A.D.)

There is no camel period. The last pictures at Tadrart Acacus were painted before camels were commonly used in that area.

The paintings reveal the great changes in the plant and animal life of the area through the centuries. They also reflect the different ways of life practiced by the various inhabitants.

Some Terms Used in Prehistoric Studies

fossil: a remnant or outline of a plant or animal preserved in rock

fossilization: the gradual transformation of a plant or animal into rock as minerals replace soft tissues

glaciation: an ice age; the formation of ice sheets covering a large region

hominids: humans and closely related human-like beings that are now extinct

half-life: the number of years it takes for half an amount of a radioactive material to break down

interglacial: a period of warmer climate between ice ages

paleontology: the science that studies life in past eras by examining fossil remains

radiocarbon dating: another name for the carbon-14 dating method

---

The Hidden Valley

The rocky mountain mass of Tadrart Acacus in Libya is a natural extension of the Tassili N'Ajjer. Like the site in Algeria, it contains thousands of rock engravings and paintings. One of them is shown in the lower left photo. The other two photos were taken at Camonica Valley, Italy. In this breathtaking valley are more than 140,000 prehistoric figures, engraved on some 2,400 rocks. It is the most important discovery of rock art to date, since the valley was isolated from the rest of the world so long.

Rock Art at Camonica Valley

In the far northern part of Italy, nestled in the Alps near the border of Switzerland, lies the Camonica Valley. Important archaeological remains—engravings and paintings—were found in the valley in the early 1900s. These works of art show that a prehistoric culture existed at Camonica Valley beginning around 8000 B.C. There are more recent images, too, belonging to the Etruscan and Roman civilizations.

In all, the valley contains more than 140,000 figures on about 2,400 rocks. With so much work done over such a long time, pictures from different time periods have been painted or engraved on top of one another.

Everything seems to indicate that the pictures have a religious meaning. Engravings of people in poses of adoration are common. There are also pictures of deer and of sun disks, basic elements in the prehistoric religion of the area. Some pictures, on the other hand, show scenes of everyday life and of the dwellings used by members of the different social classes.

Life in Camonica Valley was a world of its own, isolated from the outside world. There were a number of usual routes across the Alps, but Camonica Valley was far from any of them. That was why the valley's distinct culture lasted such a long time. Once the Romans arrived, the area was opened to trade and communication. After that, its culture started to decline. Once tourism in the Italian Alps began to develop, the valley became more widely known.

Rock Art at Alta

Along the Alta Fjord in northern Norway, near the Arctic Circle, there are paintings and engravings that seem to belong to the Neolithic Era. In civilizations along the shores of the Mediterranean, Neolithic culture flourished between 3000 and 1500 B.C. Some of the works at Alta date from that period. But most of them were made later, between about 1500 B.C. and 500 B.C. How can this be?

Glaciers covered the far northern part of the earth until at least 8000 B.C. As a result, people began to settle there much later than in warmer regions to the south. Thus, agriculture and cities appeared later in the far north than in the Mediterranean.

The most ancient works at Alta are generally those found higher than sea level. The more recent ones are lower, closer to the present sea level. There is a difference of about 85 feet (26 meters) between the higher (older) works and the lower (newer) ones.

An Unfavorable Climate
Most of the engravings at Camonica Valley have religious designs. The main elements in the religion—the deer and the sun—appear in almost all the rock paintings there. The top two photos show rock art from Camonica Valley. Below is a fishing scene in Alta, Norway. The paintings found in this fjord, near the Arctic Circle, were made between 3000 and 500 B.C. They show a glimpse of people's daily lives under the rigorous, frigid conditions of the far north.

Hunting scenes abound. At the very same time that hunting declined in the area, the paintings stopped. Bears, elk, reindeer, and whales are some of the local animals shown in the paintings. But there are also scenes of daily life, such as fishing, navigation, and ritual ceremonies. There are even scenes of farming, which was very difficult in the frigid climate.

The figures were carved in the rock and later colored, either partly or completely. The paintings at Alta have a very curious feature: the sides of reindeer and elk are sometimes crossed by a number of vertical lines. After much study, some experts have concluded that the lines represent the animals' bones.

With its extremely northern location and so unfavorable a climate, Alta appears to be the most northerly part of our planet where there was human life in prehistoric times.

Development During the Neolithic Era

Prehistoric cultures did not develop in the same way or at the same time all over the world. Thus, the Neolithic Era did not begin at the same time everywhere. There were differences of up to thousands of years between one region and another. Alta, in Norway, has the most recent paintings, such as the one at the left. Yet these paintings are much simpler than those of Altamira (*opposite page, lower right*), which were made 10,000 years earlier. The pictures at Camonica Valley (*upper right*), also less realistic than Altamira's, belong to a period between Altamira and Alta.

These Sites Are Part of the World Heritage

Caves of the Vézère Valley, located in the French region of Aquitaine. The district has 147 sites and 25 decorated caves. Lascaux, Combarelles, and Font-de-Gaume are the most outstanding caves.

Kakadu National Park, an archaeological and ethnological reserve in the far northern part of Australia. People have lived there continuously for 40,000 years. More than one thousand places in the park have examples of prehistoric art.

Caves of Altamira, near Santillana del Mar in the Cantabrian Mountains of Spain. The caves are 885 feet (270 meters) long. Of all the remains and paintings that have been preserved, the twenty figures of animals on the ceiling of the central room here are the most outstanding.

Tassili N'Ajjer, a rocky mountain mass in Algeria, with a very unusual array of plants and animals. More than 15,000 paintings and engravings from the Saharan Neolithic period are found here.

Rock Art Sites of Tadrart Acacus, an extension into Libya of the Tassili N'Ajjer. It also has thousands of rock paintings and engravings.

Rock Art of Camonica Valley. Engravings and paintings of great interest are preserved in this valley in the Italian Alps. They belong to the long period between 8000 B.C. and Roman civilization.

Rock Art of Alta, in the Alta Fjord, Norway. This is the most northerly place where there was human life during prehistory, as proven by artistic remains from as far back as 3000 B.C.

Glossary

apprentice: a student learning a craft from a master

archaeologist: a scientist who learns about the past by studying the remains of ancient artifacts and monuments

culture: the beliefs, values, skills, and social patterns of a particular group of people

engraving: a picture made by carving lines into a stone

excavate: to find or uncover something by digging or scooping out a hole in the ground

fertility: the ability to reproduce

figurine: a small carved or molded statue

fjords: deep, narrow inlets of the sea between steep cliffs; found along coasts in Scandinavia, Alaska, and southern South America

flint: a hard quartz mineral

glacier: a huge body of ice spread out over a large area

lime: calcium oxide

manganese: a grayish-white metal

monolith: a massive stone

ocher: an earthy, reddish-yellow color obtained from iron ore

pigment: a coloring material; it could be a powder that is mixed with a liquid, or a substance taken from a plant or animal

prehistoric: "before history"; occurring before human history began to be written down

relief: a sculpture on a wall or other flat surface that stands out from its background

savanna: a grassy plain with few or no trees

Index

Page numbers in boldface type indicate illustrations.

Titles in the World Heritage Series

The Land of the Pharaohs
The Chinese Empire
Ancient Greece
Prehistoric Rock Art
The Roman Empire
Mayan Civilization
Tropical Rain Forests
Inca Civilization
Prehistoric Stone Monuments
Romanesque Art and Architecture
Great Animal Refuges of the World
Coral Reefs

Photo Credits

Front cover: Incafo; p. 3: P. Vauthey/Sygma-Contifoto; p. 5: L. Ruiz Pastor/Incafo, J. A. Fernandez & C. de Noriega/Incafo; p. 7: R. Smith; p. 9: Index; p. 11: D. Hiser, R. Smith; pp. 12-13: A. Larramendi/Incafo; p. 14: J. A. Fernandez & C. de Noriega/Incafo; p. 15: P. Vauthey/Sygma-Contifoto; p. 17: P. Vauthey/Sygma-Contifoto, R. Smith; p. 18: J. A. Fernandez & C. de Noriega/Incafo; p. 19: J. A. Fernandez & C. de Noriega/Incafo, Incafo; pp. 20-21, 22, 23, 25: A. G. E. FotoStock; p. 27: S. Fiore/Firo-Foto, Schoenal/Marco-Polo, S. Fiore/Firo-Foto; p. 29: S. Fiore/Firo-Foto, S. Fiore/Firo-Foto, L. Ruiz Pastor/Incafo; p. 30: L. Ruiz Pastor/Incafo; p. 31: L. Ruiz Pastor/Incafo, S. Fiore/Firo-Foto, J. A. Fernandez & C. de Noriega/Incafo; back cover: L. Ruiz Pastor/Incafo, J. A. Fernandez & C. de Noriega/Incafo.

Project Editor, Childrens Press: Ann Heinrichs
Original Text: Marinella Terzi
Subject Consultant: Dr. Thomas F. Kehoe
Translator: Angela Ruiz
Design: Alberto Caffaratto
Cartography: Modesto Arregui
Drawings: Olga Perez Alonso
Phototypesetting: Publishers Typesetters, Inc.